S0-AHT-295

Livonia Public Library
ALFRED NOBLE BRANCH
32901 PLYMOUTH ROAD
Livonia, Michigan 48150-1793
(734)421-6600
LIVN #19

J595.799
G

Bumblebees

by Emily K. Green

Alfred Noble Library
32901 Plymouth Road
Livonia, MI 48150-1793
(734) 421-6600

BLASTOFF! READERS
2

BELLWETHER MEDIA • MINNEAPOLIS, MN

JUL 27 2007

Note to Librarians, Teachers, and Parents:

Blastoff! Readers are carefully developed by literacy experts and combine standards-based content with developmentally appropriate text.

Level 1 provides the most support through repetition of high-frequency words, light text, predictable sentence patterns, and strong visual support.

Level 2 offers early readers a bit more challenge through varied simple sentences, increased text load, and less repetition of high-frequency words.

Level 3 advances early-fluent readers toward fluency through increased text and concept load, less reliance on visuals, longer sentences, and more literary language.

Whichever book is right for your reader, Blastoff! Readers are the perfect books to build confidence and encourage a love of reading that will last a lifetime!

This edition first published in 2007 by Bellwether Media.

No part of this publication may be reproduced in whole or in part without written permission of the publisher. For information regarding permission, write to Bellwether Media Inc., Attention: Permissions Department, Post Office Box 1C, Minnetonka, MN 55345-9998.

Library of Congress Cataloging-in-Publication Data
Green, Emily K., 1966–
  Bumblebees / by Emily K. Green.
    p. cm. – (Blastoff! readers) (World of insects)
Summary: "Simple text accompanied by full-color photographs give an up-close look at bumblebees."
  Includes bibliographical references and index.
  ISBN-10: 1-60014-009-2 (hardcover : alk. paper)
  ISBN-13: 978-1-60014-009-9 (hardcover : alk. paper)
  1. Bumblebees–Juvenile literature. I. Title. II. Series.

  QL568.A6G728 2007
  595.79'9–dc22   2006005337

Text copyright © 2007 by Bellwether Media.
Printed in the United States of America.

3 9082 10531 3590

Table of Contents

Bumblebees are **insects**.

Most bumblebees are black and yellow.

Fuzzy hair covers a bumblebee's body.

antennas

A bumblebee has two **antennas**. They use their antennas to smell.

front wing

rear wing

A bumblebee has four wings.
The front wings are large.
The rear wings are small.

8

Female bumblebees have a stinger. But they only sting people when they are in **danger**.

Bumblebees live in a group called a **colony**.

Every colony has a **queen**.
Most queens are bigger
than other bumblebees.

The queen builds a nest for the colony.

Most bumblebee nests are on the ground. Some bumblebee nests are in tall grass.

Bumblebees leave the nest to look for flowers.

tongue

Bumblebees drink **nectar** from flowers. A bumblebee drinks with a long tongue.

Bumblebees collect flower dust called **pollen**. Pollen sticks to the bumblebee's hairs.

Bumblebees carry pollen from flower to flower. Flowers need pollen to make seeds.

Bumblebees also carry
nectar and pollen back to
their nest.

Bumblebees use nectar to
make honey.

Bumblebees collect nectar
and pollen all day long.

You can watch busy bumblebees on summer days. Just remember not to bother them!

Glossary

antennas—the long, thin feelers on an insect's head; bumblebees use the feelers to smell flowers and find nectar.

colony—a group of bumblebees that live together

danger—not safe; bumblebees are in danger when someone tries to bother, catch, or kill them.

insect—a kind of animal that has a hard body; most insects also have two antennas, six legs, and two or four wings.

nectar—sweet juice made by flowers; some kinds of bees turn nectar into honey.

pollen—a dust on flowers; flowers use pollen to make seeds for new flowers; bumblebees carry pollen from flower to flower to help flowers make seeds.

queen—the female bee that builds the nest and starts the colony; the queen is the only bee that can have young.

To Learn More

AT THE LIBRARY
Brennan-Nelson, Denise. *Buzzy the Bumblebee.*
Farmington Hills, Mich.: Thomson Gale, 1999.

Hazen, Lynn E. *Buzz Bumble to the Rescue.* New
York: Bloomsbury Children's Books, 2005.

Sayre, April Pulley. *The Bumblebee Queen.*
Watertown, Mass.: Charlesbridge, 2005.

Starosta, Paul. *The Bee: Friend of the Flowers.*
Watertown, Mass.: Charlesbridge, 1992.

Taylor, Susie. *The Grimy-Slimy Bug Safari.* New York:
Holiday House, 2004

ON THE WEB
Learning more about
bumblebees is as easy as 1, 2, 3.

1. Go to www.factsurfer.com

2. Enter "bumblebees" into search box.

3. Click the "Surf" button and you will see a list of
   related web sites.

With factsurfer.com, finding more information is just a
click away.

Index

The photographs in this book are reproduced through the courtesy of: Kim Taylor/Getty Images, front cover; Andrew Darrington/Alamy, pp. 4-5; David Whitaker/Alamy, p. 6; Nic Hamilton/Alamy, p. 7; Maxim Pushkarev, p. 8; Jack Sullivan/Alamy, p. 9; Scott Camazine/Alamy, pp. 10, 11, 12-13; John Bracegirdle/Getty Images, p. 14; The Image Bank/Getty Images, p. 15; Steve Hopkin/Getty Images, pp. 16-17; Chartchai Meesangnin, p. 18; Arlindo Silva, p. 19; Ace Stock Limited/Alamy, pp. 20-21.